Disappearing Address

Disappearing Address

Simone Muench & Philip Jenks

BlazeVOX [books]
Buffalo, NY

Disappearing Address
by Simone Muench and Philip Jenks
Copyright © 2010

Published by BlazeVOX [books]

Printed in the United States of America

Book design by Geoffrey Gatza
Cover art by Kim Ambriz
First Edition
ISBN: 978-1-60964-024-8
Library of Congress Control Number 2010931940

BlazeVOX [books]
303 Bedford Ave
Buffalo, NY 14216

Editor@blazevox.org

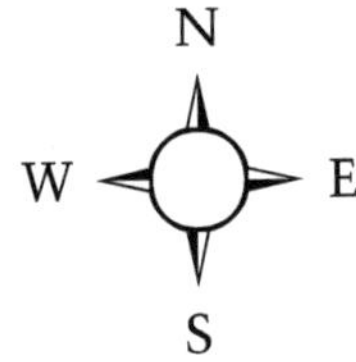

publisher of weird little books

BlazeVOX [books]

blazevox.org

2   4   6   8   0   9   7   5   3   1

B   X

Acknowledgements

42Opus: "Dear Animal Collective"

ACM (Another Chicago Magazine): "Dear Funeral Parlor Games," "Dear Director of Operations," "Dear Akhmatova" and "Dear Desnos"

Barrelhouse: "Dear Disco Dancer"

Bat City Review: "Dear Doppelganger," "Dear Alcoholic Dad" and "Dear Bitterness"(as "Dear Depression")

Bombay Gin: "Dear Dear"

Canarium: "Dear Obtuse" and "Dear Chanteuse of the Abattoir for Young Girls"

Cannibal: "Soul is all vertigo: Dear Cavafy"

Cinematheque: "An aptitude for bird: Dear Dickinson" and "Dear Player"

Colorado Review: "Dear Nothing" and "Dear Toast"

Connotations: "Dear Victorian Beauty"

Drunken Boat: "Dear Leatherface," and "Dear Philip & Simone"

Eleven Eleven: "Dear Danger," "Dear Big Pharma" and "*The weight of primary noon:* Dear Stevens"

Information Booth Anthology: "Dear Godzilla/Anonymous Caller"

Monsters & Dust: "Dear Ghost," "Dear Michael Robins" and "Dear Kim Ambriz"

Moonlit: "Dear Deer," "Dear High School" and "Dear Morrissey"

Puerto Del Sol: "Dear Sundown" and "Haptics, Not Optics"

Superstition Review: "Dear Ed Gein," "Dear Michael Myers," "Dear Film Noir" and "Dear Suicide"

A Writers' Congress Anthology: Chicago Poets on Barack Obama's Inauguration: "Dear Chicago"

Zoland Poetry: "Dear Body," "Dear Rachel Corrie," "Dear Cellphone" and *"Must I jingle my bells & kiss your bestial brow?:* Dear Baudelaire*"*

Some of these poems are collected in a chapbook titled *Little Visceral Carnival* by Nate Slawson's wonderful Cinematheque Press.

Table of Contents

Criss-Crossing Melodies
Introduction by Kevin Killian

Dear Reader, previously I have argued that collaboration tends to produce works of a significantly different quality than the separate works of their writers, but a book has come along that has made me revise my thinking. That book is the one that follows, Philip Jenks' and Simone Muench's *Disappearing Address.*

It does what few other works of collaboration manage to do: it presents a seamless surface—nearly the glass mountain of Teutonic folklore. Co-author Simone Muench has confided that this was exactly her hope when producing the intriguing poems you will be reading shortly. Far from being a patchwork of disjunction, the blend of their voices allows *Disappearing Address*, at its best, to achieve a Mozartian simplicity and transcendence. I haven't read all of the books published by BlazeVox, but this is the best of them that I know, as well as being one of the most significant volumes of American poetry of the past twenty-five years.

There has been an unnecessary prejudice against multiply-authored work. Work submitted under two names to a journal or press often will get rejected, but the same or similar work submitted under a pseudonym might get snapped right up by the very same editors. At what point does collaboration pay off?

At what point does it dissolve the individual ego and spark what Brion Gysin called the "third mind"?

Muench and Jenks asked me to write an introduction to their book partly, as she says, "to add another element of collaboration to the work." What I lack is the admirable gift for storytelling and for metaphor shared by the two poets. Their work is all the more impressive when you consider that it was at least begun when the two were living in separate cities, hundreds of miles apart. New technologies change the face of collaboration, and increase the ebullience factor which made, in the 1960s and 1970s, such New York School works as *Bean Spasms* and *A Nest of Ninnies* nearly as memorable as *Disappearing Address*.

Wayne Koestenbaum, in his admirable *Double Talk: The Erotics of Male Literary Collaboration* (Routledge, 1989) addresses the issue full on. "Collaborative works are intrinsically *different* than books written by one author alone; even if both names do not appear, or one writer eventually produces more material, the decision to collaborate determines the work's contours, and the way it can be read. Books with two authors are specimens of a relation, and show writing to be a quality of motion and exchange, not a fixed thing. Whether we call the will that produces a collaborative work inspiration, authority, or diligence, this "will" is shared." He adds, "Sometimes miserably." I don't see it like that necessarily—the misery—but to Koestenbaum's mind there's no eros without one partner who needs something and another who supplies it for shadowy, unknowable reasons. However, with *Disappearing Address*, these objections render themselves moot, thanks to the high quality of the work involved.

Koestenbaum cites Andre Gide (or rather, a character from *The Counterfeiters* who remarks): "No *chef d'oeuvre* was ever produced by several people together." That was bullshit even in the modernist era, and now in the postmodern age we have finally come to the birth of a seamless writing under which no angles or outcrops can be discerned that weren't meant to be there by the clever collaborators. (It was never a fact that single authorship produced a more stable text: Barthes told us as much in his magisterial study of Balzac, S/Z.)

I was looking for the word "different," then, to pop up in *Disappearing Address* and presently found it halfway through, inside the poem "Dear Funeral Parlor Games."

we climb
inside our lives looking for slightly more,
playing the this-one's-going-to-be-different
as we bite the Lego blue sky

The word "difference" appears more often, and dear reader I predict you will thrill to it like I did, every time it shows up. I like Koestenbaum's description of the collaborated-on text as embodying "motion and exchange," and certainly the writing of Jenks and Muench with its rapid back and forths, and its sudden redirection of address, seems to vibrate way past "motion and exchange" into an Eisensteinian roulade of montage. How fitting then, that *Disappearing Address* opens up, cinematically, in Frankenstein's tower chamber of horrors, where "anatomy is its own reward." The montagist is unreliable, not to say a liar.

> You've never looked better
> says the thief, cutting wide wild skeins of flesh.

I think the Mary Shelley thing is a brilliant way of re-staging the drama of collaboration, foregrounding both the horror of it and the purity of its scientific fervor. "It's alive, it's moving, it's alive, it's alive, it's alive!" cries Dr. Frankenstein in the Universal classic from 1931. Collaborators are walking the wild side of the street—Frankenstein scoffs at the danger element, but he's living in its moment, like a fish thriving on top of the whale's blowhole jet:

> Have you never wanted to do anything that was
> dangerous? Where should we be if no one tried to find
> out what lies beyond? Have your never wanted to look
> beyond the clouds and the stars, or to know what
> causes the trees to bud? And what changes the darkness
> into light? But if you talk like that, people call you
> crazy. Well, if I could discover just one of these things,
> what eternity is, for example, I wouldn't care if they
> did think I was crazy.

Do collaborations entered into as conceptual projects differ from the hysterical *liebestods* of previous centuries, the kind Wayne

Koestenbaum slides under his microscope? Apparently. Elsewhere the
monster imagery undergoes a sea change, remaining German but
emerging as the figure of the doppelganger. It is said that if you happen
to meet your own double, one of you will die before the year is up (cf.
Poe and "William Wilson's Secret.") Muench and Jenks aptly seize on
this myth and rewrite it so that both halves of the figure must behave
with an icy intimacy that will brook no disagreement. That they are the
same, "redundant" even, is their salvation. They are mirrors that face
each other in splendor, "criss-crossing melodies" (again like Mozart)
that "palpitate [their own] dreams." Collaboration is but one simple
slide from existence to co-existence. Why just be one ganger when you
could be two? The shadow and the figure rejoice in their mutuality, and
in *Disappearing Address* you will experience this nurturing and rich
loam as though it were a marrow running through your bones and
giving you the life to come. Each part tries to maintain individuality but
it's no use, like the old fable, once you've put on the red shoes of
collaboration, it's a dance till the very end.

Dear Doppelganger—

This is a story about co-existence.
You just moved in, shapeshifting
across the lawn, singing *be a roundabout*
to my rooftop, be a passerine to my plum tree

& don't copy yourself inside of me
lest I would not see you.

In this mirror of reticulation
your redundancy is my salvation
& capitulation. I've no choice
but to concede to you

identities I tried to hide. The dark cove

of your duplexity sings to me

in two criss-crossing melodies
that palpitate my dreams, seesawing
between static when asked,
of two isolate shadows

which would you choose: the one
with basement? Or the one with attic?

I think of the basement and attic as additional "rooms" within the body
of poetry, a la Henry James, who never met a building he didn't
compare to the attic is the eye and the basement the vulva. Dear reader,
if you've read your Frankenstein you know that not everything comes
up clover for the beloved Baron, but you lucky readers are in for an
amazing treat. I think you'll agree with me that *Disappearing Address* is
a sustained tour de force by two of the most talented American poets, or
shall I say, by a potent, enchanting and unified voice that's something
genuinely new under the sun. You won't want to miss this magic of this
labor of love.

It makes us think of all the dead
        That sauntered with us here,
By separation's sorcery
        Made cruelly more dear

        —Emily Dickinson

                        consciousness' trellis
                        wound twin convolvulus

        eave's icicles
        an attention span

                        all inextricable
                        bound in blizzard

        invite the eye
        invade the ear

                        —Ronald Johnson

Disappearing Address

Dear Dear—

I sing of your spectacular & mundane address,
put to rest nightmares of being too precious.
Those squinting throbs of double doubt caressed away.
You transcend manners with your sweet resilience we can't
contain or counter with a chemical vibrancy
of half-dismissals. No. You keep introducing wherever
we go in search of soda, something of yesteryear,
something sweet yet dreadful like sarsaparilla

in a southern diner. Would you grin on me delicately
depositing some suggestion that where there's water
there's a softer language & where there's language,
damage & you demur with the translucency
of a glass-winged butterfly that's a curious portal
into what will not & what will become.

Room One: Dissection

"In a solitary chamber, or rather cell, at the top of the house, and separated from all other apartments by a gallery and staircase, I kept my workshop of filthy creation."—Mary Shelley

Dear Nothing—

Why'd you have to cut out & make
everything come back? With glassy-
winged splendor & your circulating
center, you turn everything inside out
so it becomes itself within itself,
spinning its own airy architecture.
An observer of the supernumerary,
emperor of empirical, a note

scribbed to the abyss, we rise
& fall into the heliopause,
ejected from the stars to redress
some part of your interior, flesh
& essence. We rest in your emptiness
transfixed by a single eyelash.

"The Body is not…" John Donne – March 28, 1619
(The King Being Desperately Sick)

Dear Body—

I'd like to think, *Can I speak of love?*
Asking means nothing to you or perhaps anatomy

is its own reward. You've never looked better
says the thief, cutting wide wild skeins of flesh.

You haven't dreamed it yet? Collateral marital
damage martials us into softening dolls, grief

gluing eyelashes in irregularity. We are stuck
together. Defrosted rotten wedding cake

rubbed in our faces, a frosting façade. Eat,
be sedentary, become relationship weird,

wearied of your limping position. Motionless
veritability. Clocked by time, gash or wrinkle,

we wonder what will happen next, make reparations
to our flesh, ask tenderness to visit what can't be shut.

Repulsion distorted "organ grinder." *The night has
a thousand faces.* The face has a thousand farces.

Dear Rachel Corrie—
(1979-2003)

Hybrid of light & dirt, bright as a lemon
pinwheeling in a pitcher of blood. There is

no flesh like yours. Neither before or after,
knotted not from not knowing but beneath rubble

a spotted bird's egg floats in its blood-dress,
startled portent potential. Elaborate rung riddle,

the force of which pushed itself outward in
elegy. *You just can't imagine it unless you see it.*

Bone-black combat boot grinding opalescence.
Halted hunting scents tumescent

but bludgeon return a bulldozer's bellow,
gear slippage, rock on rock on bone.

Though she once lingered in music, skiffed
in her brain was a little story, locked & near,

shippy-thin, knocked on consciousness.
The cry I bring down from the hills belongs to a girl

still burning inside my head. When I got to the river,
she the only one living, the rest is dead.

Dear Big Pharma—

Your carefree hair remover
left only bones to address

that viscera you call witch inside you,
beside your company. You cannibalize

the Technicolor dreams of housewives,
extubation of aprons & trophies,

apoplectic regret maneuvers exhort you
to return after a century of whalebone

corsets, Poiret's hobble skirts, & command:
speak with your fan & don't say a word.

I thank you for my cenophobia & xenomanic
divination, revelate with carousel sweet

caresses, send women spinning into celluloid
caricatures all aboard the Zodiac schooner,

killer. I doubled over for you: cereal, toilet.
Bulimia is what you dream inside us,

whitening women's eroding teeth with
discipline of cotton—to soak consumption.

Feels forces, office-tuned orifice.
Offer: free shipping for a dead mistress.

Dear Leatherface—

Misunderstanding seduction
you urge your chainsaw forward

for the abnegation of travesty beneath
that mask, you mask yourself madly

in peevishness & a loping gait.
Sad stalker of all beautiful things,

king of no body. *Daddy's Sick Again*
who once politely sliced

all your red toys in two.
What to do when rural runs out

on you. It's as if you're done
but all's funhouse ricochet body farm

where fingers & tulips are planted
near the generator's trustworthy hum,

a bludgeoned gloom linger rut & rusty.
Mum's the word inside every head.

Dear Danger—

I detect sadness in your double-knit catastrophe,
          hovel of Of. Strychnine chemistry chemise

strip me of my cuirass & send me spinning into malignment.
          Manikins zombie every thread without design,

save me from your precautionary industry, haphazard affair
          with Guernica. Aphrodite held a mirror to your face,

mangled Minotaur. Guitar-slinging Texas Ranger, devotee
          to the gun church, tying bullets to hymns & humming

with teeth & garish glare, who is them there quivering?
          Who is leveraging a pick-up against a Harley?

So sorry is your song but implicit in the act is disdain,
          who says every day can't be Judgment Day? Coca-Cola

& Pop Rocks. Anthrax & an ax. These are the days
          of *gone wild*. Danger, I salute you as you mutilate.

We thought we'd play it safe & never leave, tucked
          in tiny Altamont sloppy symphonies that blast

the dawn of your lead casings, shelled but never erasing.

Dear Player—

You say I'm a naysayer for refusing your form of sorcery,

casting nothings that you "think" sexycool but all's mimicry

or synecdoche. You say *baby;* I say *maybe.*

It's just game, philopena, & when you wake,

sugar-spoon picayune, you'll find the *nothing that is not there*

drizzled with luminous language talking over itself, never listing

"listen" in its vocabulary. Just a voice—part voltage, part rain gauge,

that speaks but cannot record itself out of the past. The vinyl

history you cling to so jukebox smooth, but once I caught you

fevered in the corner of your porch, "played out" meta-master

with shrink-wrapped trousers; say it ain't so as you form

digitized lines to & from the dance floor,

guessing there is attraction in this type of execution.

Dear Michael Myers—

Witness the difference between kissing
& asphyxiation, diagnosis & prognosis.
If you find it, you can cut us in—

we'll play at the hedges & wait for you.
Or sit inside writing on a slightly steamed window
the schism between quell & cram, steel & bone;

the loud undulating plunge of one body
into two. You are the multiplier
of streetlights. Inside, housewives wonder

why a girl's writhing in the backseat of a Buick
that doesn't' belong on their street.
Further inside, housewives do not wonder

at what they know men do, then refuse to move
from the window as a cardinal explodes, leaving
a litter of crushed balloons that once held

some hopeful breath. Blood-spackled ecstasies
or choked up prosaic partner. A mask
not a man; a blue uniform that moves its emptiness

towards happiness, only to smash it
with its own insistence. Sickening regiment
& forked blue brute force, you absorb fear

until it fleshes you out, stuck on the buzz
of butchery. Your eyes, stark winter trees, flashed out
by such nothings whose lives were built

expressly for your kind of surgery, where a blade
becomes horizon & a dozen dead husbands
hang in your half-forgotten dream.

Dear Obtuse—

Be straight with me.
I love the arc of you & your arching

sentence if properly misunderstood
becomes a licensing to turn licentious.

Like the French Terror, like the waters
of the Pentecostal speaking in tongues

was just a matter of typographical error.
(& the radio's playing Lucinda's *Pineola*.)

If I read you right, would you turn away
not in dramatic disgust but more

muted, more suited to Dark&Stormy's
& a film-noir fedora jauntily launched.

Everything about you burns or spins
askance, let me love you for it. Let me

be a dictaphone recording the broken fan,
the vice of your pearl-handled voice.

Squeezed shut & it shouts, open
to full throttle & all's autumnal.

Room Two: Cross-Examination

I'm a double-dealer with a double soul.—Osip Mandelstam

Dear Doppelganger—

This is a story about co-existence.
You just moved in, shapeshifting
across the lawn, singing *be a roundabout
to my rooftop, be a passerine to my plum tree*

& don't copy yourself inside of me
lest I would not see you.

In this mirror of reticulation
your redundancy is my salvation
& capitulation. I've no choice
but to concede to you

identities I tried to hide. The dark cove
of your duplexity sings to me

in two criss-crossing melodies
that palpitate my dreams, seesawing
between static when asked,
of two isolate shadows

which would you choose: the one
with basement? Or the one with attic?

Dear Philip & Simone—

Your writing's overwrought. Too haute.
Not cuisine or couture, but chicken-legged

high-kickin' rhetoric vetted, vent,
& le vexor. French-fried car-talkers,

superspeed diesel drama. You're all dilemma
& no serenity. Prickly as Jamestown weed,

more story than history. You've been dissed
& rechristened: poet to bootlegger; writer

to gothic romancer. I just want to know:
were you in Louisiana simultaneously?

Is that a place or frequency of syllabic
slowdown? A dos-a-dos at the American Legion

hoedown where everyone's shouting bingo.
You once had a chance—sparrow & listen.

Trued by circumstance? Forget the men & shake
the dj into harmony, shake yourselves out of

a neutered dance, tremors of a doomed species.
Who locks lips to see what one is not?

Who writes themselves to save themselves,
only to find later that the whole of heavenly frame

is sickness propped up on a slouching tongue.

Dear Bitterness—

We play the game of blankness & at times

I even seek you, like coffee or what.

I can't recall, guess I got lost in you—

a head hydroplaning on its own neck

that lollygags its irony only

to dole out entropy. There's little as

vitriol as this October wind with

its aquatic chill wedged in bedcovers,

unrecycled cardboard divorce boxes

& two black banana peels. Smashed lilies

on frosted lawn. Garage sale going on.

We never intended this hostility

tucked tightly into every promise

that ever was or will be. Or did we?

Dear Suicide—

How long have you been standing in the doorway
holding a fretsaw & dreaming of indentations?

You said the body was furniture, was fixture
but we couldn't fix it. Sometimes, you the only one
talking, though neither of us narrates the way we used to;

we can't locate the colloquial phrase
to measure your presence is is-not inside us.

You move from oven to lovers, saving the date,
alive but not enunciating essence, you pile drive
a girl into ether. Ensnare a spouse in argument—

one takes car, gas, garage, & cats too.
If the sound of you is snow & the color of you

is yet to be determined, then your syntax
is parasitic gap. All talk is syllable as dynamited
sparse demarcated. Your face breaking into nickels

& stars, past tense next to an overdue library book.
Spread of the eye glassing back at the fortunate friend

who found you, lived to tell a tale of half endings,
witness to the limits of shadows that hide
in the nicked & stained couch where once we both lay.

Dear Film Noir—

We got you all wrong. You weren't the redhot rendezvous
or the bloody handprint, but the ambulance, white
in black rain, pressed against algid armors
of your electric flight.

You weren't declamation just a voice-over of a widow
droning into a dictaphone, taking notes
for a dream from scratched heads
& penciled-in threat.

Zoom to an arachnid-savvy femme fatale undressing
in a Packard, all campfire hot with her detective,
inventing the opposite
of ambiance.

Sirens hail wet against you & where you might
have been, thrust of an echo, as you offer
a collection plate for alienation
& machine guns.

Something discrete falls to the street at your periphery,
as if to suggest an inclusion or a confession
behind Venetian blinds. What's left
in your celluloid rain

is not gunfire but the glint of a gold anklet, shot of the possible
held behind its purchase & gift. The clasp's been damaged
by an insistence on a link that doesn't exist, as a row
of snow globes glistening unveil

your blackened window cracks.

Dear Animal Collective—

Your skin's gone Mahler. I'm a toxin in your throbbing.

I'm spindle to your tumble & speak fluent blue heron

& not just with the radio, no. The white-handed gibbon

goading the night resounds in caged stages. Flamingos

flare off of noble shoulders in a marriage of the exotic

with the psychotic. We are your "Animal Kingdom,"

valley without king, a castle built out of headlamps & teeth.

A furnace of wings, valence without audience. Antigenic

determinants amalgamating. This is a lesson on behaviorism.

Do you *descent with modification on the principle*

of slight variation? Do you ride humans or elation?

Dear Ed Gein—

Farmyard special of the week: hillbilly headless
stuffed with your sick absence, you slit a sliver
in my jumpsuit that says *sweet tea*. You artifice me
into defaced goat; you sell me at your little Wisconsin
grocery adorned with a sign: Eat the wicked
& leave the mild-mannered to rest
in mother's Tupperware garden. Skulk around

with razor or cleave. How strange the smell
of your own reflection, your face a cipher
with sliding doors, peer-afflicted sunspot or sunburnt
bloodspot on your pants. You once played operation,
but lost to the buzz of multiple errors, you angered
into adulthood & pulled a little bone from an innocent chin.

Weird smile glittering over the horizon
of a lock-jawed mouth, gambling to be under
sane sheets of an organized surprise, you let investigators
lead you from the guidance of *Gray's Anatomy*
in your cellar to a rubber cell carved from the hellish
real of the banal being of your truth.

Invite us to breakfast…where you serve us to ourselves
& even in incarcerated dreams we are dancing, dead.
We've finally made some plan of escape, etched in dirt
or brain—consumed in your body & what is called mind,
where all is ripe as you re-write your mother's recipes
adding nothing & deleting everything, leaving
this illness not unwritten in the margin.

Dear Director of Operations—

To strip an arm of its flesh as if it
were buckskin or petal is an act

of contagion. You once tried genocide
but forgot about the flapping mandible

inside yourself. Forgot about expandable
bodies, inflated rates for tagging tools, black-

bagged corpses who talk to each other through
chatter of what's left of their chinny-chin-chin.

Chimneys stuffed to the flue with expatriates.
Essays on apparitions & machinery. Look,

the scribes of natives stare back at you
between sliced history where heads are scattered

like handbills for a show everyone's dying to go to.
We eventually quit too, got shot or ground down.

Yeah, this was the town where we all arrived
for a test drive, to find ourselves parallel ourselves,

wishing we could wake. Instead, our bodies
scripted into this apocalyptic landscape.

Dear Chanteuse of the Abattoir for Young Girls—

Privacy is the white hood of the Nightwatchman State

where we're all audio slaves, hallucinating tunes

to disasters. Try & spin it backwards, larynx sung

sorry shovel. Reading Mata Hari's painted tongue,

weakness for men in uniforms, de- & encoding

what once was sound. Invent, envelop, espy,

& be wary of the butcher's white wax paper.

Steel bowls collect more steel bowls, frenetic clean

in that desperate room where a broom sweeping

medieval toys in a dustbin, records torture in its panicles.

Plumes plaid panic. Truncate all relation run ripped

from once was one. Soapscum melody over a murder.

Gargle scrub mouth manacles snap shut. Someone

rigged beads. Candied necklace come undone.

Haptics, Not Optics

Can't imagine how buried
it's like how under burn
is also skin—& also her.
Rinse din from follicle optical
so can't see the noise
he made when she was gone.

Like eggshell architecture, she's gone
wrong. Her good mouth is buried
beneath his inventory of noise,
light fretting a back into burns.
Where do they go with their optics,
their language of the pause? Don't let her

fret in fingers like wetting her
there across the neck *shhh* then gone.
Lips don't let anyone see publicity optical
or lantern lept longing buried
for her choice words—a daily digital burn.
He favored the colors, everything about her noise

locked him in infinite reverberate. Inveterate pink noise
a sweater makes when it empties itself of her,
buttercream borealis. Flame sucker, she burns
through lacquer through liquor *long gone*
was her whisper by the time the country buried
itself in scorched crows, rotary phones, optical

tricks of an eclipse. Is that which cannot be seen, optical
illusion or screaming at what was not said? A hexing noise
noosing its way back into what she said must not be, buried,
polished on the backporch out behind the rooms of his mind; hers
collide with the thought, sculpt it, scalp it, declare it gone.
She can hide it with some bramble, & burn

follicular. A caesura between collisions counts lips to burn-
ished skin fizzed with light. Do not rinse. This is haptics, not optics.
Not a noose in sight. They bend to flense their past to gone,
they wear their architectures well, & listen now to new noise,
a communication built of fires & hand-me-downs. *Her
hex*, he says. She hears *hoax.* He says *bitter.* She hears *better bury.*

It's not that something's gone wrong just simpler for them to let it burn.
Irradiant spicules, sunsploded ocean, refracted impluvium chimeras. Optical
bodies danced her noise, & we spill drinks in light to look at them.

Dear Ghost—

Get well with me that I might appear more sanguine
than salacious, slickened lips lost in & on
your appearance, your magical translucency.

You bear scars of lunar eclipses & I
horizoned you. Living liminal inhabited vacancy.
Transcendent flesh current. An improvised apparition

or a cloudy encounter? Transparency
or redundancy? I fell in love with your facticities.
Always, we are someone before we became

your epitome. I stand in front of you
to mourn alone & find all is drowsy
blown wrong. Carafes of empty pour out of you,

into me. We are no sorcery, the two of us
correcting each other like androids
in need of white-out fluid, an erasure

as anodyne or might we be huffing our way,
blotted on blown skiffs, needled by
the necessity of our longing. We disappear

as winter sprints spawn gusts
of that loose other we tried to rhyme with breath
but ended up in an ivory stairwell

where we acquiesced to the erotic oneiric.
We sought to walk away, or did we?
Ghost of a division, our love, our prison.

Room Three: Recollection

Dear Sundown—

I do not know which to prefer: orange crush
or grape fizz? I'm a diabetic vampire
rushing for sunglasses to elude
your corona. The bright eagerness

of your inevitability blots out
belligerent angles that tear through the day
in a granularity of luminescence
as you turn hair to fire strings in a spider

lily splendor, threading it with your undimmed
vatic collapse from season to ozone
to a violet tinctured field grazing us
with the keys to your hematology

that courses through every sound. You are
the never ever redundancy, reflecting off Martian dust
high in the failing atmosphere, into us & your
own naming that casts about in song & verse.

Dear Disco Dancer—

You're a lover not a long-timer,
Lancelot of Quaaludes
& Qiana, an answer

to the question:
how do I do your brand of simulacra?
My guesses, all imitations.

I intimate by shake
& wavering word in clubs unheard;
I high-kick to your hustle;

I'm vanilla to your medieval.

When you agree, I wonder
if pity pointed by polished boots
looks back at me.

The mirror says no to your limbs'
musings, shadow step & swivel,
livid glitter of your resurrection,

as you dance pants past imploding windows.

Spent time on earth, & you will do
the shovel, which is all in the hips'
shimmer so loosen up your holler

as you bend this way, bounce that
to "Love to Love You, Baby,"
end up on a small island gleaning

neon beams that intimate your own disaster.

Whoever wants to understand much,
must play much you said, my dazed-out
little aster as you dropped

through the dance floor
in a moon-about. Recasting summers,
this one's your seventies trip; your leverage

a line to nostalgia. Dance dance you beautiful pants!

Dear High School—

There's no chance of us
getting back together. You have disease
leased for the next five years & I want to be free

of snow globes & lobotomies lost
inside me. It's easy to caress a nightmare.
Hot pink horsey, beer-bruised & knock-kneed.

You beat a four-year carousel
out of me, while I'm still spun undone by liquor
locker whispers. Levee heave, ghostwritten intestinal graffiti.

Marked by music, walking Egyptian
through shoulder-pad hallways, bangled & feathered.
Periodic charts charred remarks. Your chemistry's all wrong

so it's bathroom rumors dealing with difference
of French-kisses versus domestic petting & who's still
a bed-wetter. This year's dead marked for a charcoal yearbook box.

Dear Morrissey—

French-kissing on a double-decker bus in a dark underpass
      wouldn't last. Wrenched from the both of us,
         crept between each that song

reminding us love is black-slatted, so *Bona to Vada*, such a grave
      roller-skater hell-bent on lack. Sweet lavish slave of self
         put yourself on the shelf? Or.

Take it back. Form a union for all shoplighters & slow-dancers
      of lyrical sadnesses. Satirical slips the tongue. The idea
         that if we were, then we might—but no.

Complicate & deliberate in your disenchanted half-beams playing
      with broken kites electing the night so it's introjected.
         Plunged shame, I'm a refracted thing

in this awful hotel, dreaming of burglaries & scissors. My hairdresser
      assassin dressed for the occasion, a personal diary refinery.
         We move beneath the disco ball,

its starburst diffraction dividing us into shimmer, shadow. Bigmouths
      criticize each other. There is no next world
         & this one's murder.

Dear Deer—

Every time I saw your sign on the North Dakota highway,
one of you showed up puffy, jut-rotted & one of you signaled

with white tail, luring us to the wilderness. What we thought was open
shut us up when everyone left. Blood rivulets bind a white blouse

to a spindly tree. Farther down the Mulberry River, fur is fevered
father damage, o you hunted! Hoofing millennia across the rotten chips

of redwood forests. Surrounded by deep-rooted trees, vertigo moved
these instinct instants collared by clothesline's linear bulls-eye as if we

were to be decapitated instead of shot. Antlers spinning through wind
in some medieval machinery. When the orange vest shot at you,

there were two other hunters too, he shot them both & heaved you
on his hood. Blood ornaments. Dent in the mental. Forest family picnics

blast Sabbath's "Thrill of it All". Clogger gargle fat, tobacco juice smear.
Fiddle, venison & beer. A homicidal father cooking on the grill.

Dear Alcoholic Dad—

Friendless & limitless. Western snow stabbing.
Turn twice & you might be; turn again
& it's dementia. You nothing but shivers
on a spurious wing slugging Rum Slings,
      performing benshi to Kubrick cinema.
         Irradiant damnation glistens

in your derangement where a blasting astronautic
blue trails into, retrieves, then guts you.

Slung down, donning drill-bitten friendships.
Benthic slug ethic. Ferment, liver's dead,
& interferon won't free you up
for an upcoming debut unless you lose
     the moustache but you can't
        save face. Bluetooth traffic

ceremony says, *Get your drink on.* Alternate ending:
run for your lover; get hit by a pick-up.

They found you forked, I mean sacrificed,
crows nipping at ideas of eyes. Friends
at the funeral hit on your girlfriend. Little
visceral carnival arranged for nothing as you
     offer entrails of the sky, lost astronaut
        locked in a loaded cloud.

Dear Funeral Parlor Games—

Between wake & woodknot
we wait, filmic substitutes for which way
to stop telling it slant, & we rate
goodbye before we cut the carotid
artery. Before we consume
our own consumption,
we play at cremation
& cut off toward chemical bins
weathering the heat of family incinerations.

We tuck ourselves inside mourners'
outfits. We arrange the party,
ill-suited for any living children
& repeat a toy is a toy is a wooden arm,
singing to the garnished hand some secret song.
Maybe if we just play along
we can insert ourselves
into something more grand
than we dreamed as kids in clown costumes.

Doubtful. New clown forms festooned
with new clown faces, just gouged
a little deeper than before as we climb
inside our lives looking for slightly more,
playing the this-one's-going-to-be-different
as we bite the Lego blue sky with cloudteeth
cut from the body of that which cannot be or receive,
bursting strained cadence of your solemn columns
where we once staged hide-&-seek.

(**From** *the Gojira Oracles & other sadsack tales of misbehavior*)

Dear Godzilla—

The parade didn't become you. You are so over the top
but this is why I love you, my atomic lover, my glottal stop,
modernist stutter step wrecker. We must stop meeting
this way! I'm splayed out by your popular culture,
your nuclear tail. Derail me with your maple-leafed
dorsal plates & heavyweight collective unconsciousness
that flattens the world beneath your postwar charm,
your angered architecture. Each step an earthquake,
Godzilla, you are so totally bombastic. I read you into
Revelations, you pretranshistoric tower crumbling as you
run towards your own disappearing future. Thunder-
bolted to a phone booth, but unable to phone home.

         Dear Anonymous Caller—

         Beware of the smallness of men on missions,
         remember not erased, but dissolving. To leave
         a residue is to leave residence of oneself.
         I shatter, but when I do the world shimmers
         then all is gone to tone, to poem, to arboretum.

Dear Victorian Beauty—

You are a filament of history
            —a gothic fragment,
            narcissus booty—

I dare not touch
your nightshade eyes
but burn for being.
            Spurned: strap me

in your harnesses that I may not
resist the raven lace of your silhouette;
rum & rosewater of unfurling hair

swings over me. I'm cataleptic
in your presence, a drunk
present under aging halls.
Billowing denial   of sexual activity
            held at bay by whalebone corset.
            Bustle-smothered lover.

Search your paramour for what whipped
yearning, your sternum humming
its bright bee garden.

Breath pollinates a population
repressed & etched into animalism,
then with demur, expulsion.

You envied ghosts their dissolving diagnosis,
& capitulated to body as ambiance,
festooned with gorgeous flesh armies—
            each an empire,
            each an arm with extended wrist.

Say goodbye
to all that's wrung
from beauty with fists
            that would forge *the yellow wallpaper*
            & call the crawling sexy.

Room Four: Veneration

Dear Dickinson, I write you each evening
dreaming of your ankle socks. Waking, what

are you not wearing today, which is not to say
thoughts of skin, empress-soft & wife-worn,

but melody or holiday, your houndstooth
fascicles woven below tumescent gaping sun

or what transpires beneath your skirt, under
your drowsy oceanic grace. Your search

for sovereign is not indecipherable but disallowed
its desired place. I envy your pollen-studded mares

for what they refused to do. Their refusals
looked back at eternity & said be damned with it.

Your witchcraft has been moored
inside of what once was. You contort,

yet still conceal. I'll be a wing
to your intuition & spell myself upon you,

shine & slant the light to your advantage,
blasts of perfect sound forever.

The weight of primary noon

Dear Stevens, tender lexicographer, let old catastrophes
become sea-clouds. With your charismatic train set,

sit this one out. Watch her pass from your garage
swaying green mousseline, her spine your residence,

luminous vertebrae. *Nînĕwâ, Al-Hadba.* You told her
the name meant that which can't be explained

or recovered. Barbaric shadows of old cars flit along
the wall, shifting the room into motion. "Gone loco"

or transit, transmission tricks. Star & petal, lifting
a blouse from her body is the mind's mobility,

its need for frisson or nightjar sadness.
It's as if that limbic jolt alone would temple

the temporal *without the oscillations of planetary pass-pass,*
though the green corn waves beyond windows

with such ardor that we may glimpse one another
because of the distance & in it, might wave as well.

Dear Cavafy, you were the shadow, the human
skull, the dear bizarre at the edge of me,

where I trace along your borders scoping
your scopophiliac tendencies. Extinguish

sadness, the past & its irrelevancies. Extinguish
him without looking & sad pass; I will walk

to you headless & reckless, hawking
stars that cling like spies to temples. Stirred,

absurd embodied panoptic skull crown. I am
fucked down like a tornado that can't see its way

out of its own recklessness, gathering madness
instead of houses. *Perhaps the light will prove*

another tyranny. Turns inside-out
inside the plank, mattering.

Your blinking eyes filled with yellow curves
& hillhouse tours, mostly bored with old

barbarisms. Now is the new frenzy—you wade
into it wondering *how quickly that dark line gets longer.*

Must I jingle my bells & kiss your bestial brow?

Dear Baudelaire, you sweat weather & wine-damp
corpses, your crepuscular braintree stems o limbic

system "gone static" neurologic lightning tests,
rest in Jeanne Duval's reclining arm, breathing out

your exile on Main Street. Skin disaster. Wind
whipped manic. You wheeled into town, witless

& nearer to nooseness. Puking electricity
out the bedroom window, joyous & free

of what scales the cerebellum, private Antietam.
Now you're just an analogy with a busted jaw

vanishing into the vast blue yaw of it, all veiny
in morning mirror inspection. Time made you

a painter of sorts, introspective & absinthe-
minded with hyacinths & hell retinally-etched.

Tethered to the hours, unsocketed orbital
instigator full of rapturous halts, revolutions

finishing in French costumes. This dance is pure
seizure in blood entombed, a ruddy seasonal bloom.

I cannot tell if the day is ending, or the world

Dear Akhmatova, cradling names beneath tongues
for future use, you held the keys to two nudes
who refuse to look directly at each other,
knowing love only at oblique angles
between military coats & cloud covers.

Gutted or starved in prison camps,
here is a kind of disaster, my dear,
next to it walks yet another.
Yet, after all the ears in the world
turned to glass & the horizon

shivered to a dead stop,
you turned starvation to a song
delivering silence
back to itself. Where things were
as they are, material & imagined,

your body a glass net catching light
where you can write lines
without surveillance or torture
but with that delicate caress of a silence
that stays & haunts the haunting.

Notes from a piano, fragments of some voice

Dear Desnos, a photograph rests in your mouth,
a grey velvet moth with a bright-eyed delivery,

cloud lumen, a ghost in the smokehouse. You
& only you *may cut the rope of this anchored ship*

leaving the horizon verse-riddled, glittering
like a bullet in an ocean, or a cigarette

burning its beauty into maritime clothing
& tossed into "corpse factories."

What's left is the strange smell of utopia rotting;
gun barrels like so many heroes' mouths.

Stink rolls down the river into towns haunted
by gouged spirits. Towns of spiders & boots

where they hummed your erasure, tumbled
over the curvature of your all-seeing eye

that bends it way back to the sea, a sublime
that crackles & sparks in an otherwise

darkened geography. A requiem on your lips.
This meeting happens in permanence.

Dear Chicago—

On election night, this grid of yours
was love blown to lava. Lit up by onions
& fireworks, a delirium of this plus that.
Did you read Max Weber's postcard about you?
Your smoky sediment; your shouldered sonata.
You are smaller in person but shimmer
on camera. Burning at a distance we walk
into you: falling glass, lake effects & electricity—
a Midwest lesson on skyscraper elation.
Perfect spot for *Henry: Portrait of a Serial Killer*
& adoptive home to Nelson, Gwendolyn & Studs.
What else do you name children living near aqueducts?

How on earth are you doing, Chicago?
Your eloquent 90/94 gouged us in two.
Will you piece that together for us, Chicago?
We still love the elongation of your body
against the frosted lake; ice is the new modernism.
Once meat. Now, you shudder
your crocuses in ground faux new-age storefronts,
stuffed abundant flatness under this lithography
of bodies. This intimate ethnography:
a human being with its skin removed.
Both city "on the make" & "on the take".
You are contradictory & quarrelsome
—as full of crooks as a saw with teeth—
yet you are also a glorious canary-filled clarity
breathing change in a young, but stumped, century.

Dear Michael Robins—

You evince immediate calm—
your incisive wit, grass sharp eyes,
surreptitious wishes
(or were those kisses?)
—they were o yes they were.
You dazzle & do so at an angle.

The best way to see a star
is to look at that corner
where it meets the dark;
the best way to see yourself
is to hear yourself
when no one else is desiring.
You split in two the *formal feeling*;
your corpus callosum lit up
like Chicago at midnight, synthesizing
every fit fright with its waking reflection.
Your face sketched with drizzle
& a blue jay's shadow,
a song in every register.

You unfold the field with silences,
unfold the silences with years,
around the empty of tree stuck folds
of every & nothing at all
& find a dreaming word for everyone.

Dear Kim Ambriz—

With your mezzotint smile & your seagrass
sway, you shake cocktails & our bodies
with soul that's your soul too

though an inconsolable vapor
bathes your loosening self—
a Gal Costa album looping

in the background of your body.
Kim Ambriz, where do you go
when sleep is fitful; when the world

appears as a woodcut
—a broken carousel
imprinting itself on sleeping figures

& it seems no mind would bear
but right there where your eyes mythologize,
humming with pearl-light over the dark bar.

How could anyone not be rapt
by your wavelike grace, backlit by mirrors
& orange liqueur? Want to learn

everything about you, your falling horses,
your Aztec codices; what you do
& do not say? What you play that makes

all dance & forget, mute our pain,
filling mouths with fricatives,
reminding us the self is a tender labyrinth

full of palaces & jazz
as your kindness turns sadness
to spangle & we lean to your lunar flame.

Room Five: Valediction

Dear Cell Phone—

Bacilli reticulate to bacilli.
You're breaking up & "is that me?"

with hands free, or the coroner passing out
Hello Kitty covers & other pink accessories

that might signify some connection, concoction,
irradiant "Genius of Love": *I'm in heaven*

with the maven of funk mutation. Whereas, for me,
I like the motion of the rotary. It's better than rosaries

or some half-baked born again heaven to be next to
them headsets & hymns. Cause of death was not rapture,

but noise toys, a cerebellum rupture. Speed dial or die.
Beguile in bramble, scramble & it becomes chatter.

It's no longer about connection but transcription.
A stenographer's nightmare, daze of dictation

dilates to attaching meaning. You were sent before
we turned off the recorder & now we wonder

who will reorder us? Who will translate into song
the static from our makeshift selves, our scattered cells?

Dear Toast—

My most reliable & delicious friend, you taste best
with Prosecco & a midnight make-out

on New Years Eve, making every kiss count
with final ounce of liquid light bouncing off

your meniscus. Never faltering at a stranger's troubles,
fermenting, transfiguring snag to song

as you hail seeds in the champagne light
of late afternoon. You are the something-soon.

We turn into you, trued by your pure immanence
& caress a thigh in the grape-dark humidity

of your fecundity. You are the imaginary,
that moment before what can flash between cup & lip;

the confluence of past nostalgias with the body's arc
toward radiance. You swivel under projected spokes

of the unspoken, pouring light & dark all over us
in slow mimosa motion. Bodies fluted,

spilling finale into finality, saluting
without end, our sparkling demise.

Simone Muench's Thanks
Much gratitude to the following people for their loveliness, inspiration
and constant support: Richard Every, Jackie White, Hadara Bar-Nadav,
Wesley Kimler, Don Chatham, Jesse Muench, John McSween, Retta
McSween, Clare Rothschild, Tom Lynch, Lauren Levato, Francesco
Levato, Jason Koo, Tim Rutili, Joshua Clover, Bill Allegrezza, Lanko
Miyazaki, Stephanie McCanles, Brandi Homan, Kristy Bowen, Lina R.
Vitkauskas, Jessi Lee Gaylord, Nate Slawson, Reg Saner, Marilyn Krysl,
Fred Sasaki, Jacob Knabb, Joel Craig, Greg Purcell, Nate Zoba, Sarah
Gorham, Nickole Brown, Karyna McGlynn, Susan Slaviero, Heather
Galan, Ray Bianchi, Robert Zessar, Kevin Stacy, Matt Jencik, Michael
Robins, Larry Sawyer, Dean Rader; and, to my Danny's dance crew for
what would I do without you, *shimmy shimmy ya*—Kim Ambriz, Sarah
Long, Melissa Grubbs, Philip Jenks, Lana Rakhman, Catherine Blauvelt,
and Bill Mondi. Special thanks to the editors and staff of the journals
that supported our (and others) collaborations, Sarabande Books,
Switchback Books, Cinematheque Press, Illinois Arts Council, Robyn
Schiff and Kevin Killian for their generosity, Michael Anania for his
mentoring, Robert Archambeau for his shiny mind, Ed Roberson for his
dazzle, and Geoffrey Gatza for his unfailing niceness and fantastic press.

Philip Jenks' Thanks
Simone Muench: for making every successful aspect of the collaboration
possible and saving my life more than once.

Carrie Olivia Adams, Kim Ambriz, Teresa Bair, Zach Barocas, John
Beer, Paul E. Blackburn, Rachel Chamberlain, Joel Craig, Grace Dillon,
Sarah Dodson, Dusie Press, Dutch Art Institute, John Dziennik, Eric P.
Elshtain, Richard Every, Jack Fisher, Flood Editions, Ben Friedlander,
Betty Gabriel, Forrest Gander, Jonathan Goodman, Chris Glomski,
Janna Gornik, Annie Guthrie, Neil Hagerty, James Hatch, Matthew
Henriksen, Lisa Janssen, Denda Jenks and the Jenks family, Devin
Johnston, Kevin Killian, Jacob Knabb, Cybele Knowles, Yves
Labissiere, Robbie Lee, Jennifer Moxley, Laurette Liesen, Daniel
Martinez, Christopher Mattison, Andy McCleod, Karyna McGlynn,
Sasha Miljevic, Tanja Miljevic, Josh Miller, Tom Moss, Simone Muench,
Rian Murphy, Michael Newton, Michael O'Leary, Peter O'Leary,
Daniela Olszewska, Greg Purcell, Herbert Reid, Michael Robins, Chris
Ross, Chris Roth, Fred Sasaki, Larry Sawyer, Leslie Scalapino, Jennifer
Scappettone, Robyn Schiff, Mike Signs, Nate Slawson, Eirik Steinhoff,
Chuck Stebelton, John Tipton, Elizabeth Treadwell, Lina Ramona
Vitkauskas, Joshua Marie Wilkinson, Jonathan Williams, Leila Wilson,
Allyssa Wolf, Zephyr Press, Robert Zimmerman.

Simone Muench was raised in small Louisiana towns and the Ozarks in Arkansas. She is the author of *The Air Lost in Breathing* (Marianne Moore Prize for Poetry; Helicon Nine, 2000), *Lampblack & Ash* (Kathryn A. Morton Prize for Poetry; Sarabande, 2005), and *Orange Crush* (Sarabande, 2010). She has been a recipient of two Illinois Arts Council Fellowships, a VSC Fellowship, the 49th Parallel Award for Poetry, the Charles Goodnow Award, the AWP Intro Journals Project Award, the Poetry Center's Annual Juried Reading Award, and the PSA's Bright Lights/Big Verse Prize. She received her Ph.D from the University of Illinois at Chicago, and is director of the writing program at Lewis University where she teaches creative writing and film studies. Currently, she serves on the advisory board for Switchback Books and UniVerse: A United Nations of Poetry, and is an editor for *Sharkforum*.

Philip Jenks was born in the south, grew up in Appalachia and came alive in the Pacific Northwest. Now he's haunting Chicago. His poems have appeared in *Chicago Review, Typo, Fence, Cultural Society, H_NGM_N, Canarium, LVNG*, and elsewhere. He has published two full-length volumes of poetry, *On the Cave You Live In* (Flood Editions) and *My First Painting will be 'The Accuser'* (Zephyr Press). He also published two chapbooks – *The Elms Left Elm Street* (Plane Bukt) and *How Many of You Are You?* (Dusie, 2006). His collaboration with Simone Muench, *Little Visceral Carnival* was published by Cinemateque Press, 2009. He also collaborated with Sasha Miljevic, publishing <u>Distance</u>, an ekphrastic hybrid of prose and poetry (Dutch Art Institute, 2009). He recently completed his third manuscript, *Colony Collapse*.

Made in the USA
Monee, IL
07 July 2026